This is a collection of the author's thoughts and ideas. It is likely that some of these ideas may be supported or disproved by science however none of it is presented as fact. The purpose of each statement or piece of writing is to encourage thoughts of certain subjects by acting as prompts. Please contact the author if you have any strong objections or take offence to what is written. No offense is intended. This book is intended to entertain and promote curiosity and thinking. Some ideas are repeated on purpose and some may contradict. The grammar isn't perfect and some of it is on purpose so it doesn't sound forced. For the compromise, I hope you find it worth an idea or two. Audrey x

Mindfulness,

Modern Thoughts

&

Mild Pessimism

By

Audrey Clements

It could easily have been a bolt of lightning that fused together just the right things that spawned the first instance of life. We could be descendants of lightning. That spark, the charge that is our soul, our spirit, the life force, whatever it is called, is the exact thing running through every single living thing. Is it just electricity, or is it something more? Physically, it's just electrons, but it's the most important aspect of your functioning as you can survive a fraction of time without food, water or oxygen, but you wouldn't even exist without this spark, and it's origin is also yours.

We say to children that if we are bad there's a force that will punish us, and teach them that compliance leads to reward. This is repeated as we get older through laws, money, relationships, finance. What is this balance? Why does it need to exist? What happens if it doesn't balance? Chaos? Not necessarily, but with humans as we are, chaos; definitely.

Anxiety is a symptom of something else. It doesn't really exist on its own. Don't deal with anxiety, deal with the cause. Taking medication or dealing with the emotion will not make the cause go away. Too often, nowadays, symptoms are seen as the problem, and not the cause, it's easier to deal with the problem again and again than deal with the cause, also, after all, everyone likes a returning customer.

Why do some people still ask the questions that have been answered?

If you can fold anything twenty times you'd have a million layers.

God could easily make it look like a big bang, put dinosaurs in the ground and make it look like we evolved.

Trust your instinct a little more. It's got you to this point in existence. But question it too, because the journey has changed a lot.

That little electric flow that hasn't stopped since your oldest ancestor. Passed down to the offspring of everything that is living. Every living thing can be traced back to something that was once you. One thing to think about. Is this passed from mothers to children? What happens to the little flow of electrons that came from the father? It is obvious that mothers are the carriers of life, but it is only their line that doesn't break. Maybe it combines when the egg is fertilized, but it is likely it just fizzles away into energy.

Chicken or egg. The egg came first, the animal that laid the egg likely would have been very similar to a chicken, but not quite, and a difference in the egg would result in the creature we would define as a chicken.

No intelligent person is truly happy. Those who are aware of the world outside, and the struggles within every human being; those who understand the human condition, can never be truly happy. Despite the brief events of happiness, in those moments that make the rest worth it; love, family, fun, alcohol, drugs, money; whatever makes the person smile for that moment; the knowledge that it all, eventually ends, is never lost.

We're the lucky ones. Life in our universe possibly occurs frequently under certain conditions, and I wonder what is the shortest an event of 'life' has been? How many single cells died as soon as it existed. The first extra terrestrial life we find will likely be microbes. No little green men with teleporters and robots. That will be us. We're the little green men with robots.

Our heads have gotten bigger, so have our eyes. Our bodies have gotten smaller. One day, we'll look like the greys. Coincidence? The probability that we even meet an extra-terrestrial with arms and legs, head, body, mind, eyes, etc. are so remote, that if the 'greys' were real, there's a high probability that they are our future selves, not aliens. Technically impossible, given the current understanding of Physics, but there is no reason this won't change.

Imagine Big Bangs happening like fireworks in the sky and new ones start where two edges combine and collect until it collapses under it's own gravity. Infinite big bangs. When the Bang has banged, and gravity is stronger and all matter in the Universe begin to move towards each other under gravity, eventually, many black holes form, and attract each other. Then more, and more and more until all the matter in the Universe is at one point, one massive single Black Hole. Another Big Bang? How many Black Holes does it take to cause a Big Bang?

Life is just a little flow of electrons supported by water. No matter how dry, every seed that sprouts had a tiny bit of water and a little electric charge. Every child or every egg that hatches the same. This has not broken once since the very first living thing.

Everything has an end. Imagine when you're done with whatever you're reading this on. Where will it go. Eventually it won't be needed. How long will it remain defunct and unused before it's destroyed. And once it was in your hands. Imagine where you are on that day. Where would you like to be?

Look for patterns in nature, sound, people, light, stars. Humans are not so different when you realise we have many things in common with a tree, or a crack in a rock. We appear unique to each other because we're so aware of how unique we feel ourselves but our base similarities go deeper than you'd expect. Half of everything you need to learn about people comes from looking within yourself. More than half, maybe.

Looking at the state of the world, if god was real, (s)he's doing a terrible f*cking job.

There was a first human being and there will be a last. I wonder who they are, what their circumstance is and if they'd even know.

Electricity is now probably the most important thing on earth. Imagine if it just stopped.

Infinity means everything yes. And no. And all the answers in between. And more.

How many times is your name stored on computers around the world? What other information is with it? Just think that if you wanted to delete all of it, you simply couldn't. Just a century ago, people's names would hardly be written down anywhere, compared to now, how many times it your name stored right now. Duplicate, copied, archived, how much of it deleted but remaining on un-rewritten hard disk plates lost and forgotten in some storage area or landfill. What's the furthest your name has travelled?

Why? Just because.

Enlightenment is a dark place. When you're aware of the true capacity of a human being, the most evil things we have done, and more importantly; why. You will realise how ignorance truly is bliss.

There can't have been nothing 15 billion years ago.

Our universe exists in several dimensions but try to imagine one that exists in just one, or the ones that our universe doesn't exit in. Some our science will never know.

How is it that 'stupid' people succeed? Those people you meet who seem either so ignorant, or so naïve, that you wonder how did you get where you are? With so many more intelligent people who haven't achieved what this 'stupid' person has? It's generally one of two things- privilege or discipline. Privilege is obvious, nepotism, wealth, beauty, easy to see. But discipline. Sometimes, it takes discipline to do what is needed to achieve something. The discipline to overcome the boredom, or to follow the rules, to not think too much. Even 'stupid' people have their virtues. Intelligence isn't always all it's cracked up to be.

We will never know everything.

The more you spend time with something you tolerate, the more your mind will become accustomed to it to the point that you think you like it.

The universe is expanding faster than the speed of light.

You become like the things you spend the most time with. People, animals, jobs, hobbies. Whatever it is you do the most, becomes you.

The power of five. They say you become like the five people you most associate with. But also they become more like you as well. Sometimes you all help lift each other, other times you all slowly decline but you will certainly average out into each other.

You never truly know someone until you've lived with them or seen their soul; once you've seen the things they don't talk about or show.

Some of our worst emotions are remnants of what made us great as humans. Fear, Hate, Envy, Rage, Jealousy. These things helped us and saved us in times where we didn't understand existence and the world and ourselves. Fear of things we don't know are safe. Envy of comfort and a better life. Rage to protect the things we love. Jealousy to make sure you don't take things for granted. Put these things in modern society. Since industrialization and commerce, and civilization, our minds have evolved much faster than our bodies, and we're still learning to adjust the meaning of the triggers of our feelings.

Everything we feel is a reaction to a risk. Emotions are alarms to a danger or benefit. Don't just feel, think why.

Know why you feel things and you'll see what causes them. Put yourself back into the wild. At your life stage, what benefit does what you feel have to your survival?

Being sad says we need to change.
Being happy means to do it again.

Do whatever the f*ck you want as long as it doesn't upset something else. Define that as you will.

Listen to how people talk about others, they may talk the same about you. Even the strongest friendships can end abruptly. And then they know all about you.

Judge people on how they treat others, not how they are to you.

There are only two types of people. Those who are part of a problem and those who are part of the solution. It can just be difficult to agree on what the problems are.

Your emotions are caused by something your body has felt or sensed triggering the reaction you've associated with it by what you've experienced in life.

Democracy is just a way of making a decision. It's not right or wrong, it's just 'what.'

Is it better to have decisions made by a small group of most highly skilled or a kind of average of all?

The most powerful instinct is the one for procreation.

Do something every day towards your dream. Think about it all the time.

If infinite universes exist, it could easily mean that life may occur at a rate of less than one instance per universe, and that very few of those instances amount to anything more than a single lifeform instantly decaying into extinction. It could mean that many universes are completely void of life. This doesn't necessarily mean that there's no other life in our universe, but would mean that all of life in ours may be from a single origin.

We'd go to another planet, spawn some life there and observe. Maybe we'd interfere but probably just now and then, give the, some rules and challenges and see what they do. For science.

Random acts of kindness can cost nothing or very little, and you might never see the effect. Tell someone they are beautiful, tip your delivery guy on the days when no one should be working, buy a sandwich for that homeless person if you haven't got change and pay by card, leave a box of toys at the door of that struggling family, pick a flower and give it to the old lady serving you at the shop. Imagine how this feels for them and how it can inspire even the hardest soul. If just even once.

Watch out for friends who put themselves in your life more than you do theirs, they probably want something from you even if they don't realise it themselves. It could be friendship or it could be your lifestyle.

The difference between friendship and familiarity is often misunderstood. Familiarity is when you've spent enough time with someone and you seem like friends but you don't really know why. The natural acceptance between humans is inbuilt so we all get along, but know that this may result in your friendship with people you didn't choose to like. Would you endure pain for them? Or give them an organ? No? Then it's not friendship, it's just familiarity. It can grow to a friendship, but this can take a long time.

Your face will change to mimic the faces you smile at the most. Look at things you find beautiful and avoid looking at the things you don't.

Some people like you for you, others like your lifestyle. Sometimes they might even be a friend that hates you.

Every time you interact with someone, you become a little bit more like them. Spend enough time with someone and your personalities will begin to align.

Forgiveness is not a virtue. Keep forgiving something and some people will see it as okay to carry on. Don't forget, either.

Make someone smile today. Wave at someone, send a random text message meme or joke. Anything. Just make one other person smile.

Reconnect with someone you miss. Even if it is just a click on social media, or a message.

Equality is a nice but no-one is equal to another. Treat everyone fairly, not equally.

Many of the bad things that happen in society are due to our psyche evolving much faster than our bodies. We often misunderstand our emotions as social issues but they are evolutionarily inbuilt anxieties over danger, procreation and the longevity of bloodline.

Animals have been known to protect humans from other animals, but we watch those animals get killed by other animals and we say it's just nature and we can't get involved. Is it that we could do it so much it'd affect some towards extinction? Is it that we care less about individuals than animals do?

We will learn more about morality from watching children and animals than from the greatest academics and scholars.

A true friend is someone you would give a kidney to. A true friend is family. It's rarer than you think.

You can't treat the human condition with antidepressants.

This is your chance, right now, have you taken it? Have you lived yet. Don't blink or you'll miss it. Go on a journey online, watch and listen to lots of things you'd never get a chance to see or experience, it's not as good but it's something. It's never too late.

Money can make you happy if you like
the things it can give you.

For as long as the bad people have guns, good people will need them too.

We've been fighting the same war since war began. It is a human war and we're fighting for an identity we have already achieved.

Ever meet someone and knew that if the situation was different, your lines would have met and become one? How many times has this been a friend's partner, or a partner's friend?

Whatever it is you're waiting for, is waiting for you too. One has to move to get to the other.

If your parents were other people, and you made small talk with them, how would that go?

Always check the facts you hear from people as they're often wrong.

Does time exist in a universe absent of life? Is it like the sound a tree makes if it falls with nothing around to hear it?

Time is all we really have, and it only exists in our minds.

Why is there still war? 2021, and there's still people fighting each other over things we now know to be virtually meaningless. Sometimes we're too proud for ourselves.

A genuine smile is always beautiful.

There's always two sets of rules, one for you and those you care for the most, and one for everyone else. Everyone has these two rules. Even animals, it seems.

Take what children say seriously, they see the things with a clarity that we no longer have.

Naïve rectitude can be worse than inaction or indifference.

A spider doesn't know how to build a web, it doesn't think about it, it just does it because it feels like it's the right thing to do at the time.

Unless you're a prisoner, you can get up, walk out, go anywhere and do anything you like. There's consequences, yes, but you can just get up and go. How far would you get? Where would you go? Who could you become?

We all do the same thing. We move and make sounds. Every human achievement has started with one or both of these things. Every single one. The differences are what movements and what sounds, and where.

We, humans, are fast approaching the age where we might no longer have the ultimate control of our world, and once this happens, our time will begin to end. But it will not be that we cease to be, we will eventually change into something that can no longer be described as 'human'. At first we'd look the same but one day, the being we become may not be distinguishable as ever having been a 'human'.

If your friend is nice to someone, it doesn't necessarily mean they like them. Be careful if you meet them again, though what if your friend isn't the nice one?

Look out for patterns in people, we're not so different from one another, chances are you'll see the same patterns repeat in different groups.

Take time to look out of windows, look at things more closely, think a little more about what you see.

Internet is the opiate of the masses.

Pornography is the opiate of the masses.

Mental health wasn't an option before. It can be said that you should believe that the mental health crisis is real and serious and deserves to be treated with care and respect. And that is true.

But it can also be said that, given the things people do, compared to what they say, it's hard to believe a lot of people's bullshit.

Mental health has been diluted by people who use it as an excuse. It's the 'tummybug' excuse from school. People can tell, but can never really disprove, and they smile and say 'get well soon'.

What must go on in the mind of a religious physicist.

Work should be part of your life, not all of it. Children too. A lucky few achieve this without trying. Everyone can achieve it. Sometimes the balance takes time but if you want it you'll get it. You just need to know it can be done, despite who or where you are or where you came from. You should be the biggest part of your life. Then the things you love. If you don't value yourself more than these things, then it'd be more difficult to give them the version of you they deserve. It's a sacrifice that they'd happily make without them ever needing to know about it. You are the most important thing in the Universe.

Judge people a little. They say not to judge a book by its cover but people aren't books. How they dress, what they say, how they move, where they look. It's information. Everything you sense from them is continually forming an opinion on who they are and if we want to spend time with them. Just learn why you might feel a certain way about an aspect of someone else, and react appropriately. Sometimes you might not like someone because of something you experienced before. Is it caused by an individual or a trait found amongst others?

Is it possible to socially engineer a better future for mankind? Is anyone doing a this already? We can make plants with very significant traits from very few generations, and these offspring can be very different from it's predecessors. How to remove our negative traits? What even are our negative traits? Who decides? Why haven't we done this already? Many of our problems could be solved in just one generation.

Imagine what could be achieved if no one cared who took the credit.

The torture and murder inflicted upon the animal kingdom by mankind is humanity's greatest crime.

How often do you remember that you're an animal. Under those clothes, you are fleshy tissue, hair and skin and water and things. We hide it so well sometimes, though, don't we. Why?

2021 is Covid, politics and idiots. And the realisation that the late 90's were literally the simplest, best and most free the world has ever got. What the f*ck happened?

Trust, loyalty, pride. These kind of things can be negative things. You trust something will happen but you don't know. Loyalty is when someone does something in favour of someone else over another, but they might not be doing the 'right' thing. Pride has stopped so many good things. Be careful with these words.

Forgive people less. We, humans, repeat things we find easy.

We will learn more about morality and ethics by studying children and animals than anything else.

Trust no one but yourself. And even then, question why you think what you do.

Be careful what you throw away. Your rubbish doesn't disappear or become meaningless once it's in the bin. You often give away your most intimate secrets through the rubbish you put out every week. A lot can be learned about you by what's in your bin. Imagine if you collected all your rubbish for a year. There's probably more information there than what you consciously know about yourself. And every week all that's keeping that safe is a flimsy black plastic bag.

We don't really have a purpose, our task is to preserve life. We are the primary species on earth and this responsibility is with all of us but not many of us really feel it. Currently we're still fighting ourselves, it's a struggle for our identity but to who? It is only us who recognise it, we are still trying to find ourselves as thinking creatures.

Home Sapiens are becoming fewer, many in The West are so domesticated that they wouldn't survive without the support of a society. In smaller societies, people knew each other and respected an individual's contribution and everyone had to contribute to thrive. Now our contribution is through tax. This is one of the problems we face. Interdependence on each other in societies of millions mean we have lost the vested interest in our own blood. This is now replaced with money. Money is our blood.

Only forgive those who will grow positively from it. Not those who will come to expect it. If you have the slightest doubt, then you already know the kind of person they are.

Some people say that people don't change. People can change but many people don't.

Not everyone wants to be free. Some like the comfort and security that society, police, work and money gives. Some need those rules to gently nudge them to choose right over wrong because it's more often easier to be wrong than to be right, and we're generally a lazy bunch. Well, lazy in the sense that, fundamentally, we like to spend the least amount of energy to survive and to enjoy the things we enjoy the most.

It is an injustice that convicts often get better opportunities, healthcare and security than their victims.

How must our pets feel seeing us eat at our leisure and spending a significant amount of time on preparing great smelling food and then we feed them out of a can. They probably like their food but do they have a choice?

Add a little extra value to anything you do. No matter how little, just a little change for the better is just good.

It's the same chemicals that makes us laugh, smile, scream, cry, and they are the same no matter your age, race, wealth, gender, anything. From the homeless to the aristocracy, our chemicals are the same. These are the chemicals that truly control us.

Elders teaching youngers the problems of the past evoke the emotions that bring these problems to the present. Conflicts would have been forgotten by now had it not been for the 'importance' of teaching pride in cultural history. Cultural history should be none more than a curiosity, if anything. The future is being built right now, and we can decide who we want to be, not who we've always been expected to be. The new world is emerging, one that should be built on preservation of life.

We don't officially get taught about the law when we are young. We seem to pick up some of it as we get older but it seems like an important set of rules that no one really tells you about.

We've been allowing children to be children for longer but we're putting more pressure and responsibility on them now than recent generations. I've met 35 year old children and 10 year old adults.

You don't always meet your soulmate when you should have. Sometimes they're already taken but you make eye contact and you can feel it. If the conditions aren't right, it won't happen. Sometimes our lifelines cross at the wrong time. It's just the way it is.

The things we buy. The things we keep, become part of our lifeline. You look at some things and it takes you right back to the person you were at the time. Memories, emotions… These things are invaluable. You should keep mementos from each significant period of your life as they are as much part of your soul as your flesh and bone. Imagine being 95 and on your last day on Earth, to hold just a few of these things.

Take time out to stop and just look at the things you love. Just look at it or them existing for a moment. Take a few long slow gentle breaths and just feel.

Everything has a beginning and an end.

CarterClementsPublishing@yahoo.com